Creatures of the Deep

INTERESTING INVERTEBRATES

Heidi Moore

Raintree

www.raintreepublishers.co.uk
Visit our website to find out more information about Raintree books.

To order:

☎ Phone 0845 6044371
🖹 Fax +44 (0) 1865 312263
🖳 Email myorders@raintreepublishers.co.uk

Customers from outside the UK please telephone +44 1865 312262

Raintree is an imprint of Capstone Global Library Limited, a company incorporated in England and Wales having its registered office at 7 Pilgrim Street, London, EC4V 6LB – Registered company number: 6695582

Text © Capstone Global Library Limited 2011
First published in hardback in 2011
Paperback edition first published in 2012
The moral rights of the proprietor have been asserted.

Edited by Megan Cotugno and Abby Colich
Designed by Philippa Jenkins
Picture research by Hannah Taylor
Originated by Capstone Global Library Ltd
Printed and bound in China by CTPS

ISBN 978 1 406 22641 6 (hardback)
15 14 13 12 11
10 9 8 7 6 5 4 3 2 1

ISBN 978 1 406 22648 5 (paperback)
16 15 14 13 12
10 9 8 7 6 5 4 3 2 1

British Library Cataloguing in Publication Data
Moore, Heidi, 1976-
Interesting invertebrates. -- (Creatures of the deep)
1. Marine invertebrates--Juvenile literature. 2. Deep-sea animals--Juvenile literature.
I. Title II. Series
592.1'77-dc22
A full catalogue record for this book is available from the British Library.

Acknowledgements
We would like to thank the following for permission to reproduce photographs:

© Kevin Raskoff/ MBARI p. **22**; Corbis pp. **8** (© Ralph White), **25**, **26** (© Bettmann); FLPA p. **6** (Minden Pictures/ Norbert Wu); Image Quest Marine pp. **12**, **15**, **17**, **18**, **20**, **21**, **29**; naturepl.com pp. **24**, **28** (David Shale); NOAA p. **27**; Photolibrary pp. **5** (Phototake Science/ Kathleen Crane), **10**, **19** (OSF/ Scripps Inst Oceanography); Photoshot p. **4**; Science Photo Library p. **14** (Thierry Berrod, Mona Lisa Production); SeaPics.com p. **23** (Lia Barrett); Shutterstock p. **7** (© Jeffrey M. Frank).

Cover photograph of Giant Tubeworm Colony reproduced with permission of Corbis (Ralph White).

We would like to thank Michael Bright for his invaluable help in the preparation of this book.

Every effort has been made to contact copyright holders of material reproduced in this book. Any omissions will be rectified in subsequent printings if notice is given to the publisher.

Disclaimer
All the Internet addresses (URLs) given in this book were valid at the time of going to press. However, due to the dynamic nature of the Internet, some addresses may have changed, or sites may have changed or ceased to exist since publication. While the author and publisher regret any inconvenience this may cause readers, no responsibility for any such changes can be accepted by either the author or the publisher.

CONTENTS

Some words are printed in bold, **like this.** You can find out what they mean by looking in the glossary.

GIANT TUBE WORMS

In 1977, a group of scientists made an amazing discovery. They were exploring the deep sea near the Galapagos Islands in the Pacific Ocean. They were diving to depths of about 2,500 metres (8,200 feet).

Underwater springs

In this cold, dark place, the scientists found hot **springs**! The springs come from underwater vents, or gaps in the ocean floor. These vents release heat, steam, and gases from below Earth's surface. Before this, scientists thought that no living things could survive here. But they found many deep-sea dwellers living near the vents. There were huge clams, blind shrimp, and white crabs.

A deep-sea explorer takes pictures of life in the deep.

Giant tube worms live near deep-sea vents.

Monster worm?

One of the most unusual creatures found near the vents was the giant tube worm. It is a large white worm with a red plume at the top. The plume is a feathery part that sits on top of the body. Giant tube worms can grow up to 2.4 metres (8 feet). That is taller than a human!

Field of flowers

With their red plumes, a swaying cluster of giant tube worms looks like poppies waving in the breeze. Some people think they look like tubes of lipstick.

LIFE IN THE DEEP SEA

Life in the deep sea is difficult. Little to no sunlight makes its way down there. At some depths, there is total darkness. The water is very cold. There is also intense water **pressure**. The further below the surface you go, the harder it is to survive.

Adaptations

Many deep ocean dwellers have **adapted** to this tough **habitat**. They have unique features that help them survive far below the surface. Some creatures, such as deep-sea shrimp, make their own light. Special chemicals (substances) in their bodies glow. This is called **bioluminescence**. Have you ever seen a firefly? They have bioluminescence, too.

This comb jelly glows with bioluminesence.

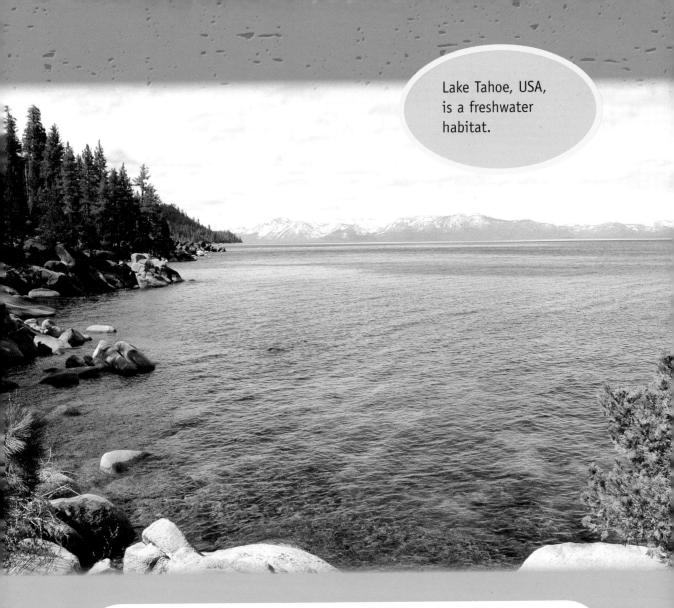

Lake Tahoe, USA, is a freshwater habitat.

Freshwater, saltwater

Freshwater is found in lakes and rivers. It contains very little salt. Seas and oceans have saltwater. These are known as **marine** bodies. Oceans cover about 70 per cent of Earth's surface. They are important habitats that are home to many amazing creatures.

DEEP-SEA VENTS

Deep-sea vents are a strange place to live. They are very harsh **marine habitats**.

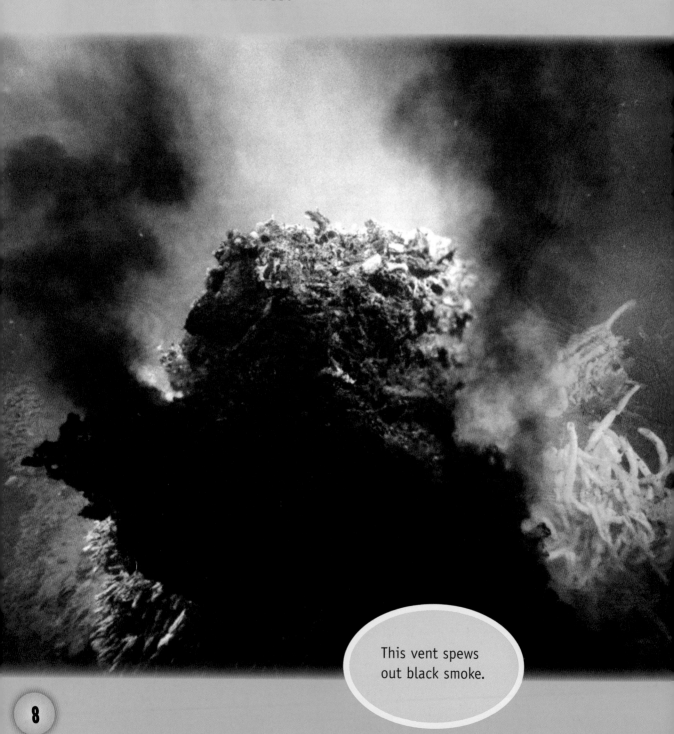

This vent spews out black smoke.

Hot and cold

Hydrothermal vents have extremes of heat and cold. The word hydrothermal means 'hot water'. Water from the vents can be almost boiling. That is hot enough to cook an egg in a few minutes! But near by the water is very cold.

Poisonous gases

Hydrothermal vents spew many gases, such as hydrogen sulfide. Some of these gases are **toxic**, or poisonous. The vent openings range in size from 13 millimetres (0.5 inches) to more than 1.8 metres (6 feet).

Animals living near the vents **adapt** to these unique conditions. So far, scientists know about more than 300 types of creatures that survive near hydrothermal vents! Somehow these creatures do not get cooked by the hot temperatures.

Underwater chimneys

Some hydrothermal vents are called black smokers. They spit out black smoke like chimneys. Sometimes iron in the smoke stains the tube worms orange!

BOOM OR BUST

Scientists once thought that it would be too hot to survive near **hydrothermal** vents. But the heat they provide can mean life or death for some creatures.

On and off

Sometimes the vents switch on and off. When the vent stops releasing gas, the animals cannot survive. When the vent switches back on, new animals move in. They grow very quickly. These animals have learned how to take advantage of the right conditions.

Tube worm barbecue

Scientists found one extremely hot hydrothermal vent in the Pacific Ocean. They recorded temperatures up to 403°C (757°F). The water was so hot it burned the giant tube worms' flesh! So scientists named this site Tube Worm Barbecue.

Plant-free zone

There is no sunlight deep in the ocean. That means plants cannot grow there. Plants need sunlight to make their own food.

sulfide-rich hot water

vent fish

vent

vent

octopus

galatheid crabs

giant tubeworms

Many living things make their homes near a vent.

limpets

giant white clams

NO EYES OR STOMACH

A giant tube worm is roughly what it sounds like. It is mainly a tube.

The body of a tube worm

Giant tube worms have three main parts. Its main part is a long, thin, worm-like body. This part sits inside a tube made of a hard material called **chitin**. The third part is the plume, which sits on top of the body. The plume is red because it is filled with blood.

Giant tube worms do not have a stomach or a mouth. They also do not have eyes. There is no need for eyes in the deep ocean. After all, there is no sunlight down there.

The red plume on top of a tube worm's body is filled with blood.

Baby tube worms

Tube worms produce new tube worms by **spawning**. A tube worm releases **sperm** and eggs into the water. The sperm and egg combine to create a new tube worm. After it hatches, the tiny tube worm swims down to a rock and attaches itself there to grow.

A tube worm's body has three parts.

plume

tube

trunk

Fast growing

Giant tube worms grow quickly. They can grow up to 84 centimetres (33 inches) per year.

POISON FOR FOOD

Giant tube worms do not have a mouth or stomach. So how do they eat food? The answer is that they don't! But they still need a source of **energy**.

Giant tube worms' energy comes from hydrogen sulfide. This is one of the gases a **hydrothermal** vent releases. You might have smelled hydrogen sulfide before. It sometimes wafts out of sewers and smells like rotten eggs. Hydrogen sulfide is very **toxic** (poisonous) to humans. But to **bacteria** living near the vent, it is food! Vent bacteria use hydrogen sulfide to make energy. The bacteria, in turn, supply energy to the deep-sea dwellers living there.

This is a close-up image of bacteria.

Getting energy

This process happens inside a giant tube worm's body. A tube worm is filled with squishy brown tissue loaded with bacteria. Blood inside the tube worm's plume takes in hydrogen sulfide and then sends it down to bacteria in the tissue. The bacteria feed on the hydrogen sulfide and produce energy for the tube worm. The giant tube worm lives off poison!

This tube worm lives near a hydrothermal vent.

POMPEII WORMS

There are many amazing deep-sea **invertebrates**. Invertebrates are animals that do not have a backbone. Humans have a backbone. Worms do not. Worms are a type of invertebrate. Many of the strangest **marine** invertebrates live near **hydrothermal** vents. Life in this **habitat** leads to interesting **adaptations**.

Other worms in the sea

Giant tube worms are not the only worms in the deep sea. A Pompeii worm has a mainly grey body. It is covered with thin, red **gills**. The gills look a bit like a porcupine's quills. Pompeii worms are much smaller than giant tube worms. They are only about 10 centimetres (4 inches) long.

In two places at once

The worm's tail end sits in very hot water of up to 80°C (176°F). This is the hottest water temperature that animals can withstand. Only certain **bacteria** can live in hotter water. But the Pompeii worm's head rests in much cooler water. The Pompeii worm has **adapted** to life in two habitats at once!

This is a
Pompeii worm.

DEEP-SEA MUSSELS

Other interesting **invertebrates** make their home near **hydrothermal** vents. Like giant tube worms, some of these deep-sea dwellers have **bacteria** in their bodies. The bacteria take in vent gases such as hydrogen sulphide. They use chemicals (substances) in the gas to make **energy**. The deep-sea dwellers live off this energy.

Mussels are a type of **shellfish**. They have millions of bacteria inside their **gills**. The bacteria use energy from the vent gases and make food for the mussels. Mussels quickly move into new active vent sites. In fact, they are often the first creatures to turn up there. They can also filter some food from the water. When the vent stops releasing gas, mussels can survive for a short time.

Some vent mussels grow as large as a human hand.

Mussels cluster on rocks in the deep ocean.

Spider-mussel?

Mussels have a weird way of moving. They shoot out a strand, like a spider's web. The sticky strand latches on to a rock or other hard surface. Then the strand shortens and pulls the mussel along.

VENT CARNIVORES

Other animals living near **hydrothermal** vents get food in a different way. Some of these deep-sea creatures are **carnivores**. Carnivores are animals that eat other animals. Carnivores are also called **predators**. The animals they eat are called **prey**.

Crabs and shrimp are common vent predators. They feed on mussels that cluster near vents. Brachyuran crabs are round white crabs. They live near hydrothermal vents in the Pacific Ocean. They are fearsome predators, feeding on giant tube worms, mussels, shrimp, and even other crabs!

This round white crab feeds on vent mussels.

Scaleworms are covered with pink overlapping plates.

The scaleworm

Another common vent predator is the scaleworm. They do not look like any worms that live on land! Scaleworms are flat and covered with overlapping pinkish-purple plates. The plates look a bit like pink crisps. Scaleworms attach to black smokers, or underwater chimneys (see page 9). Scaleworms are also predators. They eat tiny **crustaceans** (shrimp-like animals) called copepods. When the vent stops working, carnivores like these cannot survive. They rely on other animals for food.

OTHER INTERESTING INVERTEBRATES

There are many amazing deep-sea **invertebrates**. Some live near vents, and others prowl the ocean floor.

Bloodybelly comb jelly

This strange creature looks a bit like a human heart. Bloodybellies range in colour from purple to deep red, but they all have a blood-red stomach. Scientists think the red colour is an **adaptation**. Bloodybellies are **predators**. Some of the creatures they eat have **bioluminescence**. The striking red stomach hides the glow from these creatures. This keeps the bloodybelly from attracting predators itself.

The bloodybelly jellyfish seems to glow red.

This glass sponge rests on the ocean floor.

Glass sponge

These strange animals look like white lace tubes. In fact, they are made of glass! The glass sponge forms thin layers of **silica**. Over time, the silica builds up into a complex structure.

Deep-sea squat lobster

This animal is not really a lobster at all. It is a type of crab. The squat lobster has very odd eating habits. It eats wood! Deep-sea squat lobsters munch on trees and other wood pieces that fall to the ocean floor. They even feast on shipwrecks!

EXPLORING THE DEEP SEA

Interesting **invertebrates** have **adapted** to life in the deep ocean. Humans have not. We cannot survive for long in the deep sea. The extreme cold and **pressure** are deadly to humans.

There are many reasons to explore the deep sea. Scientists want to learn about the amazing animals that live there. But they cannot just swim down and look around. Even a wet suit and scuba gear are not enough. To explore the deep ocean, scientists need special vehicles and equipment.

Scientists

Many scientists study the deep sea. **Marine biologists** focus on all living things in the ocean.

A marine biologist takes pictures of deep-sea life.

The bathysphere

One early deep-sea device was the bathysphere. It was a **sphere** made out of steel. Two people could fit inside. The steel withstood the intense water pressure. Inside was an oxygen tank so the people could breathe. In 1934, two scientists dived down to 923 metres (3,028 feet) below the surface. At the time, no one had been that far underwater.

This bathysphere is being launched into the ocean.

MEET ALVIN

Today, many cool tools help scientists explore the ocean floor. Deep-sea **submersibles** travel far underwater. They are like **submarines**, only smaller. Some submersibles stay attached to boats or submarines on the surface. Long hoses supply oxygen or power to the submersible. Others operate on their own. Scientists fit inside and control their movement.

A submersible named *Alvin* helped scientists explore **hydrothermal** vent systems. It made the first trip down to the vents in 1977. This submersible still makes more than 150 dives a year. It has been rebuilt many times. *Alvin* played a key role in the discovery of giant tube worms.

This is *Alvin*, the submersible.

Alvin has been rebuilt many times. It continues to help scientists explore the deep sea.

Sunken sandwich

In 1968, scientists used steel cables to lower *Alvin* into the water. Suddenly, the cables snapped. *Alvin* tumbled to the ocean floor. Luckily, the three crew members on board got out safely. But their lunch was trapped inside! Eleven months later, scientists brought *Alvin* back up to the surface. To their surprise, the sandwiches had not spoiled! They were not exposed to sunlight or oxygen so far underwater.

SAVING THE DEEP SEA

The oceans are so large, it may seem like we do not need to worry about them. But we do.

Danger from people

The deep ocean is Earth's largest **habitat**. Today this unique habitat is at risk. **Pollution** threatens to change or harm the deep sea. (Pollution is harmful waste.) Human activity has led to **global warming**. Over time, the temperatures in the deep sea may change. This would upset the delicate balance of **hydrothermal** vent systems. Vent dwellers have **adapted** to the exact conditions there. If the conditions change, they may not survive.

The ocean is home to many amazing living things, such as these sea butterflies.

Pollution poses a serious threat to the world's oceans.

More to explore

It is important to protect the deep ocean. There is still a lot to learn about it. We know very little about many of the amazing animals that live there. Many deep-sea dwellers have not been discovered yet. Scientists know more about the surface of the moon than the deep sea!

GLOSSARY

adapt change to fit an environment

adaptation feature developed over time that helps a living thing to survive in its environment

bacteria single-celled living things that can only be seen under a microscope

bioluminescence light given off by a living thing

carnivore animal that feeds only on other animals

chitin hard material found in the outer skeleton of invertebrates

crustacean living things with a hard exoskeleton, two pairs of antennae, and a pair of legs on each segment

energy power to move, change, or grow

gill organ through which a fish or underwater animal breathes

global warming changes in temperature that are taking place around the world

habitat place where a living thing lives. Living things adapt to their habitat.

hydrothermal having to do with hot water

invertebrate animal without a backbone

marine having to do with the ocean

marine biologist scientist who studies plants and animals in the ocean

pollution harmful waste

predator animal that hunts other animals. Some deep-sea predators hunt for food along the ocean floor.

pressure weight or force that pushes against something

prey animal that is eaten by other animals

shellfish sea dweller with a hard outer shell

silica mineral used to make glass

spawning releasing eggs into the water to be fertilized

sperm male seed that fertilizes an egg

sphere evenly round object like a ball

spring source of water that comes from the ground

submarine vehicle built to explore underwater

submersible small underwater craft

toxic poisonous

FIND OUT MORE

Books

Exploring the Deep (Project X Hidden Depths), Chloe Rhodes (Oxford University Press, 2009)

Classifying Invertebrates (Classifying Living Things), Francine Galko (Heinemann Educational Books, 2009)

Ocean Life (World of Wonder), Carolyn Franklin (Book House, 2008)

Websites

ngkids.co.uk/inside_scoop/1104/giant_jellyfish_ invasion_
Read about a giant jellyfish invasion swarming in Japanese waters.

news.bbc.co.uk/cbbcnews/hi/newsid_6930000/ newsid_6935100/6935143.stm
Pilot a submarine through deep seas to discover new underwater creatures. But beware of the volcanic vents!

www.deepseaconservation.org/issues/climate.php
Learn more about how global warming is harming our deep seas.

INDEX